Surface Deep

ENEAZER LAYNE

XULON ELITE

Xulon Press Elite
2301 Lucien Way #415
Maitland, FL 32751
407.339.4217
www.xulonpress.com

Paperback ISBN-13: 978-1-6628-5610-5
Ebook ISBN-13: 978-1-6628-5611-2

Dedication & Acknowledgements

To all the women who have allowed me to speak life into you and gave me an audience as I poured from my core in real-time while I was **Be**coming: Thank you for seeing the value of my life, embracing the words spoken to you and trusting me with your hearts.

To my nephew Diego Wyatt for being the catalyst, consultant and coach to finally bring this work to fruition. Thank You for helping me Rock My MOXIE!

To my saintly mother for being the conduit of life for me, for loving me and for praying for me.

To my two phenomenal sisters, Doristein and Frieda, your support, encouragement and honesty means everything to me.

To my Only Begotten Son, Andrae, who is the first student, and my five Gorgeous Grandsons, I Love You to the Deepest Depth, Forever.

In memory of my forever 22 daughter, JuJuana Nichole (Nikki). I carry and keep you alive in my heart forever.

Finally, to my husband who covers, encourages, affirms,
cares and loves me in word and in deed.
You are my Rock!

Table of Contents

Surface Deep Endorsements

I Loved your book; it gripped my heart and I cried and was moved throughout with your story and the process of the 4 stages of Growth as a woman! You Are Remarkable!!

Surface Deep...the Evolution of You is a must-read for every woman. Eneazer Layne grips your heart from the beginning, urging readers to dig deep into who we are by sharing her personal journey and has a beautiful way of challenging you to look into your soul through the four seasons of life. Her book is unapologetically grounded in faith. She shares that each person is made to manifest in this world. It's up to you to look in the mirror and say "Yes" to God's Purpose for your life. Will you answer the call to "Show Up and Show Out?"

Kathy Lambert - KBL Impact Partners, Inc.

I've not only watched the evolution of Lady E (My Mom) but learned from the evolution! As scientists study the caterpillar through their evolution to the beautiful butterfly, going Surface Deep to find the 'I Am in Me' is just one lesson I've applied to my Life and Evolution. Get ready to Rock Your Moxie!

Only Begotten Son–Andrae Blissett, Sr.

No wise person would start a journey without a roadmap or a guide.

Surface Deep...The Evolution of You provides clear directions and road signs so you can successfully navigate your journey towards a more powerful and successful life. The book is filled with imagery and insights that are the key to transforming your thinking and your life. Eneazer Layne's message is refreshing and offers hope to the discouraged, lost, and stuck but also serves as an inspiration to those believing they were made for more. Layne provides a mirror to help you see who you can become, not just who you are today. If you are ready to dig deeper, go further, and become the best version of yourself, you must read this book. You won't be able to put it down.

Dr. Lethia Owens–Gamechangers International

What a refreshing peek into the world of someone who is yet becoming ...

Lady E walks us through the corridors of history with authentic transparency, providing us with the hope of a better day while growing from the inside out. Let's celebrate the gift that is Lady E.

Bishop Robert E. Martin Jr.

Introduction

A lot of time has been wasted,
wandering in the wilderness of life...
Going around in circles doing the same thing over and over again.

It was during an awakening period of my life that I wondered and asked myself these questions:

What is the meaning of this?

Why am I in the same place now as I was then?

I remember saying, "Something is wrong with this picture of my life; Somebody has been lying to me." I was getting older and wiser, but my situation wasn't changing because I had accepted and embraced life as I had come to know it based on what I had been taught.

Everything that was going wrong in my life was my focal point and in the forefront of my mind. I was emotionally bankrupt and convinced that this was as good as it would get. Even though there were wins in my life, they eluded my conscious mind because subconsciously I was convinced that I was not enough, I was not capable of greatness, I didn't deserve better, I was under-educated and unmotivated. I dared not dream because of these self-deprecating thoughts and limiting beliefs. Oftentimes I thought, "If this is what life is all about, I don't want to breathe another breath." After stepping over the line to be god of my own life and attempting to take my own breath away, I woke up. It was in the moments after this I believe I started living intentionally. It was as if I was on auto-pilot. It was as if I was in the birth canal, on my way to *becoming*. This new birth did not come easy and so many times I doubted myself, saying "I can't," "I don't know how," or "I quit," but I had a will to win–even in my weariness.

It was between the ages of 42 and 58 that I began to experience many awakenings. I began to notice things I had never paid attention to. I began to feel the weight of things I once shrugged off and also laid aside weights I no longer wanted to carry. I asked God to circumcise my ears so that I could hear only His voice and open my eyes to what He wanted me to see.

At 58 years of age, I inquired about getting certified as a life coach. The representative asked me specific questions to gauge whether I would be a good candidate for the program and gave me a hard yes that I qualified. She then told me the cost. It was at least three times the cost I had in mind, but I knew this was the program and team I wanted to be on. I wanted to grow, I wanted to defy every limitation that had been placed before me. I joined the Maxwell Leadership Team, and became a certified coach, speaker and trainer. What a win, right? As I went through the courses and studied, I realized much of what I was learning, I already knew – but I didn't know that I knew what I knew. I hadn't tapped deep within to unearth my intellect and understanding. Even though I knew that coaching and pouring into women was my passion and sweet spot, it was also during my 58th year of life that I realized I had been coaching, teaching and mentoring for almost 40 years. I was somewhat despondent because I felt I should have recognized this years ago. I felt that so much time had been wasted and it was too late to start building a business and to learn how to be a more effective leader of a nonprofit organization.

This 58th year was a pivotal time in my life as this was when I began to write this book which is written to help you awaken your consciousness and consider your life on a much deeper level so you can redeem the time here on earth, taking nothing to the grave worth utilizing.

I had an identity crisis most of my life which is one of the most debilitating dilemmas a person can have. It was paralyzing and crippling and was stunting my growth. I am blessed to have lived to find resolve and absolution as I experience countless flashbacks, good and bad, that serve as reminders of things I have endured and wins I didn't acknowledge. There is so much more depth to each of us that we have not tapped into or that we've tapped into but haven't extracted out *all* of our essence to share with the world and fully *Be.*

I believe that as you read *Surface Deep… The Evolution of You*, you will begin to have flashbacks, as I have had, and remember things you've forgotten, put things behind you that you've remembered and held on to that do not serve you well, embrace possibilities as you take on new perspectives, reintroduce you to yourself and get to know *You.*

Sometimes you have to be reminded of what you haven't forgotten.

Surface Deep…the Evolution of You was written from an anatomical and physiological perspective to activate you to live everything between your birth and death (your dash) well aware and with intention. Be advised that this book only scratches the Surface of the evolution of you. I invite you to be the doting participant in your own life while reading and fill in the birthings of thought, ahas and revelations at the end of each season in this book.

Though there are many chapters in our lives, Surface Deep is written in seasons because each trip around the sun brings us back to a season we have already experienced. Life has many seasons, from seed and conception to birth and then the cycle of seasons begins again. Life as we know it re-cycles.

No matter your age, whether you're 18 or 58, it's never too late to start. There's no wrong time to start living intentionally, authentically and on purpose. I hope you will be willing to choose to LIVE in every moment of your remaining life to leave a legacy of wealth to those who are watching and mirroring *You*.

As I have come to *know* myself, so shall you *know You* from the **Surface** to **Deep**.

Season 1

The Journey

Do you remember the day you were born? Have you ever heard anyone say: "I remember the day I was born?" No. That's because no one remembers the day they were born.

The day you were born, you had the innate fortitude to poke a hole in the embryonic sac in which you were nourished, where for the gestational period of nine months, if you were full-term, you developed and resided comfortably. As the embryonic fluid left the sac in which you had been swimming, you found yourself in a state of suffocation—no water to swim in and you had never taken a breath. Yet you lived. You were in a state of darkness and suffocation with no place to go because the vast difference in size between the portal of the birth canal and your form made for a seemingly impossible feat. *You*, who knew not who you were, but knew enough to persevere with determination, pressed onward and went through the process of being born—of *Becoming*—because you had a will to win and you were already destined to win.

The journey began when your father and mother became one with each other, and *You*, a seed, was planted.

You… were the one out of millions that was viable.

You… were the one that didn't fizzle out in the race to reach your destination—to be.

With reckless abandon, *You* attached.

You penetrated and fertilized an egg in your mother's fallopian tube.

You knew you couldn't stay there. And because the tube was too small to support your imminent growth and there would be no access to nutrition there, you continued to move upward and settled deep within her womb. If not, you would have perished, and your first failure would have been your final one.

You were determined, *you* had a goal, *you* refused to be a statistic and didn't have a diagnosis of failure to thrive. You were like a little acorn that had been planted deep in the earth and held its ground.

Biologically, the cells that formed at that point were called a zygote. I will say that You were never a zygote, rather that zygote was *You*. Even at that early stage, the essence of your existence, everything that would define you—your sex, facial features, disposition to disease, race, hair color, etc.—was set. Even if there were some chromosomal anomalies, *You* continued on your journey. *You* didn't quit. At this point, it was just a matter of time. The process for the manifestation of *You* was coming about.

Evolving

For a thing to evolve, there has to be a process. Process doesn't happen overnight. It evolves over a period of time. Patience can only have her perfect work with time. You were not ready to be born a day or three after you were conceived. It was necessary for you to go through a gestational period to develop, grow and mature. There were three (3) 90-day trimesters during which miracles and the progress of your process was taking place. Each trimester proved crucial for wholeness.

Your survival largely depended on your carrier—your mother. It was necessary for your mother to protect you by choosing the right diet, taking her vitamins, abstaining from alcohol abuse, nicotine products, drugs, physical abuse and minimizing her stress levels. Hundreds of thousands of people had mothers who did not observe the above mentioned and were careless to a fault, and it is possible *You* were one of the people who survived anyway. *You* survived and are still here reading this book right now because *YOU* had, and still have, a will to win.

Throughout the first process of your evolution, as you were positioned deep into the womb, your form was not what you would become. You began to morph into what would look like a lima bean and began to sprout from there. Your presence was made known because you had stepped into your mother's space and made her very uncomfortable. Hopefully, in spite of the fact you made her nauseous, she welcomed you with an open heart and immediately fell in love with the thought of you, even if there were adjustments that needed to be made in her life. At this stage, you had no say in how she would care for you and didn't have a say in whether she would cut you off by aborting you. The fact that you are here no matter her state of mind, or stage of life, shows you were allowed to stay planted and rooted.

In this first trimester alone, two of your major organs were in place. Your lungs were formed, your heart started beating and you had a spinal cord. By the end of the third month, your head, which included your facial features, hands, fingers, feet and toes, had formed. You were well on your way! Guess what? You didn't wait to see if your life would be cut off before growing. You didn't wait to evolve. You continued to occupy and move toward your expected end.

In the second trimester, the evidence of your gender was identifiable. You were covered with skin and fine hair, your legs were growing between your feet and body, and your arms were growing between your body and hands. Your digestive and immune systems were forming. Your fingers and toes were more defined, your senses were developed, and you were moving and repositioning at will.

In the third trimester, all of your vital organs, except your lungs, were functional and you were growing exponentially. At this point, your lung and brain development were most crucial. You were able to hear music and recognize your mother's voice and the voices of those who were in close proximity to her. By the end of this trimester, you were making your mother very uncomfortable, and you, too, were becoming uncomfortable. Because of your rapid growth, your movement was becoming limited. It was at this time that you had to get into position to move from the place where you'd once resided, learned voices and grown accustomed…that place of familiarity.

Completing the entirety of the gestational period is necessary for the development of any healthy being. Perhaps, your mother may have been ill or struggled with abnormalities in her body and was not able to carry you full-term, or you are one of multiple births, or by some unforeseen phenomenon you were prematurely born. The proof that you were meant to BE is evident because you are here. You, though tiny and underdeveloped, went through a harrowing experience and fought to live and breathe. And still, you continue.

Lima Bean

A family member, whose name I will not divulge, had a desire to have a child. For years she was not able to conceive and her family, especially her grandmother, who is known to have a direct line to God, prayed for her to bring forth a child. After years of patiently and impatiently waiting, she informed her family that she was pregnant one Mother's Day. Because she'd had such a challenging time conceiving, she wanted to wait until she had gotten through the first trimester to reveal the good news to others. The fetus remained viable through the first trimester and the journey continued.

With much joy, her family and friends anticipated the completion of forty weeks of pregnancy and the arrival of what the grandmother called "her joy" to make way into this world. But something happened at twenty-two weeks. Lima Bean poked a hole in the embryonic sac and released the fluid in which he was swimming. This was not good news. The young woman was told there was little hope and even was encouraged to abort Lima Bean (she gave them a hard no). After a few days in the hospital, Lima Bean said: *I have got to get out of here... This ain't working!*

A baby boy was born and he came out feet first. Weighing 1 lb. 2 oz. and measuring the size of his father's hand, things looked bleak. It would take a miracle for him to survive. Much prayer, ginger care from the doctors and Lima Bean's will to win had to be a concerted effort. He not only survived, but he is also thriving today—eight years later. As he was in a hurry to come into this world then, he is always ready for an adventure and runs all of the time now.

Poised To Emerge

From the time of your conception to the time of your first breath, a lot has happened. You were about to emerge as a total human being from the beginning with a "Thought in the mind of God" and a seed planted. Wow!!! *You* are amazing because from that seed to conception through the process of evolving into ***You... You Are!!!*** No matter the circumstances of your birth, whether you were planned and highly anticipated by two parents who anxiously awaited your entrance, whether you were a welcomed oops, or whether you are a product of rape, molestation, prostitution or promiscuity, *YOU* made it. YOU Are! Again, no matter the circumstances, good and favorable or bad and indifferent, your circumstances did not keep you from "Being." Your father planted the seed in your mother. You remained viable, and as long as your mother allowed you to stay there and was willing to house you, *you* thrived and grew. Here is the thing... *You* had the innate intelligence to thrive unconsciously. You unconsciously thrived.

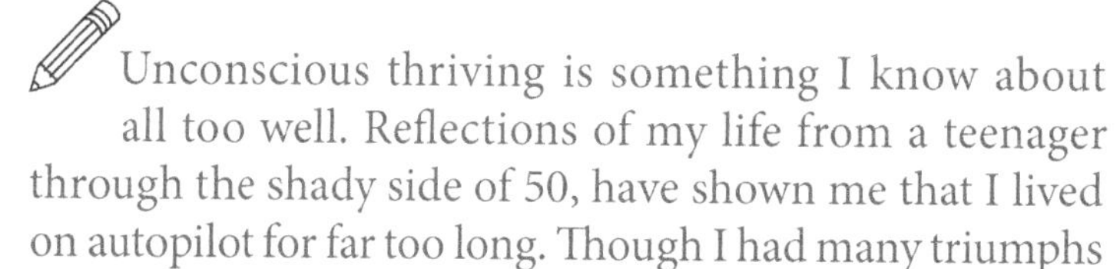

Unconscious thriving is something I know about all too well. Reflections of my life from a teenager through the shady side of 50, have shown me that I lived on autopilot for far too long. Though I had many triumphs in life, it seems the tragedies are what I remembered and allowed to permeate my mind and memories. There were significant life events I didn't remember until recently—especially the wins. When I had a win, in my mind, it was as if I shrugged it off like this good thing was a mistake, and sooner or later, God was going to realize I was an imposter, or it was a win that wouldn't last.

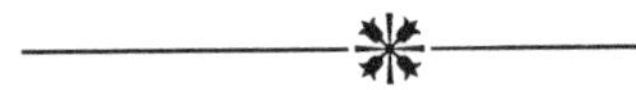

Unconsciously I continued to thrive and do even more that proved I was so much more than I realized. On the ***surface,*** I had it all together. I had it going on. But ***Deep,*** I had no idea who I was or the impact of my purpose.

How many rebirths had I experienced?

How many births had I pushed out?

How many people watched me "BE" me to the core and were inspired to "BE" and bring forth, as well?

Today, my rebirth lies in the awakened consciousness of my reflections and intentional acceleration of exploits to come. If you're reading this book, you are holding the proof in your hand and a seed is being planted for exponential growth.

And so, it is now. There are many births that must take place in your life and in the lives of others *you* touch. Failure to thrive is not an option, or is it? *You* choose. The fact that *you* continue to live is an indication that there is more growth in you. As the day came when you said to yourself, "I like it here, this is home for me, but if I stay, I will die," so it is as you continue to live, breathe and grow that you will make the choice of rebirth.

You have come through many trimesters and many periods in life where you've become comfortable in your process. Many of you have become uncomfortably comfortable. You have stretched your dwelling place until there is no more room to grow. A move has to be made. Time's up! Death is imminent; emotionally, psychologically, spiritually and physically, if you are not willing to position yourself to emerge through the eye of the needle or that dark tunnel that is claustrophobic, uncomfortable, tedious, time-consuming, painful, scary and causing you to suffocate. You defied the limit of time for a human to hold their breath. Afterall, you had yet to take your first breath and you were no longer swimming.

Whether you are giving birth or being birthed, you must assume the position and… Push… Emerge… Bring Forth… Come Forth!

Your destiny is calling you and tugging at you, saying, "come on." That thing that you're good at and do so well and you're so passionate about; that dream or vision you see that keeps you awake at night; your gift that has already made room for you, your destiny and God's purpose for your life that truly defines who you really are and is the narrative between the date of your emergence (birth) and the

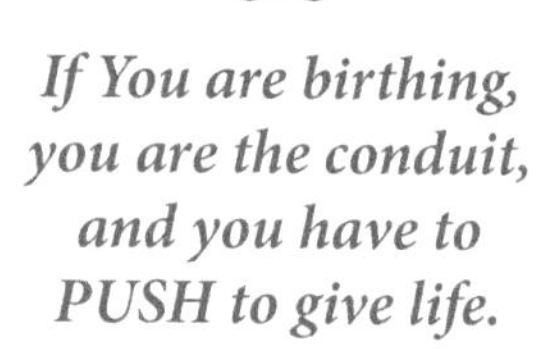

date of your exodus (death) is driving, pushing, tugging and pulling on you to understand that there are many processes and in the fullness of time there's an end to all processes. It is time for you to realize that the place you have been in is no longer big enough for you. You have outgrown it. Your lungs are now developed, your brain has absorbed the knowledge needed and your heartbeat is in sync with God. Now you are in the right position. *YOU* are poised to emerge. And you experienced your first birth—your first season in life.

At the moment of your birth, you had defied odds and were a living miracle. *You* evolved from a seed to a zygote to an embryo to a fetus to an infant… a living human being.

On the ***Surface,*** you are beautiful in the eyes of those who see you and hold you. Even if something about you seems flawed, they see you as perfectly flawed. At the emergence of you, you had a clean slate, and everything ***Deep*** within you to attain endless possibilities remains to be cultivated and seen in the impending chapters and seasons of your life.

Birthings of Thought

Season 2

The Awakening

Look at *YOU*! Oh my, *You* made it! *You* did it! Welcome to life and a new normal for you.

You have successfully completed the first season in your lifetime and entered a new season. The manifestation of You is tangible with limitless possibilities. You cannot yet perceive what those exploits will be because you're still unconsciously thriving innately. You were born with a blank slate and your story from this point is being written from the chalk of those whose care you are in. God began your story when you were planted and now you are in the hands of those He entrusted you to.

This new normal isn't so comfortable. Life in this new place has given all of your senses—touch, sight, sound, smell and taste—a whole new meaning. While you were in the womb, you were very comfortable and cozy and you only had to move because you had outgrown the space you were in. *You* endured a journey that was uncomfortable and seemingly impossible to go through, but you made it! *You* made it through the eye of the needle.

Such is life. We go through the process, the metamorphosis of *becoming* and then it seems that yet again, another cycle of *becoming* begins.

After being in a suffocating, claustrophobic situation, you made it through. And then you felt something you'd never felt or experienced before: Air.

Breathing not Swimming

You immediately reacted to a new environment to which you had to quickly grow accustomed. You felt air touch your skin for the first time. You experienced cold for the first time—a far cry from the comfortable 99.7-degree temperature you'd known for nine months prior.

The little hairs on the skin you were in during the second trimester stood at attention, and the nerve endings directly underneath your skin made a connection with your brain. You took your absolute first breath, and again, your brain reacted and caused you to use your voice as you cried for the first time. This cleared out your bronchial passageway to Spirit and Breath. Your lungs, which carry and circulate that air and deliver oxygen to your heart which circulates your life's source, began to work in concert with other major organs. Guess what: this was your first time multitasking. *You* innately knew what to do and how to react. *You* met the challenge and *you* won!

Stimuli

Getting acclimated to a new normal isn't easy. It is uncomfortable and often painful not to be in the place you once knew. *You* adapted to the shock of the unknown coming into contact with your developing senses. There were adjustments to be made in your new environment. Your brain had to identify and respond to everything.

Your Senses

The first sense you felt was *touch*. The moment you emerged, you felt someone's hands on your skin. You had never been touched by human hands and the drastic change from the warmth of your mother's womb yielded to air. *You* innately breathed for the very first time. You also may have experienced pain for the first time if the doctor, midwife or person who delivered you smacked you on your butt. Isn't it interesting that one of the earliest sensations you had was pain?

You also experienced the *touch* of your mother's warm embrace. Amid all of the shock to your senses was comfort and the nurture of the mother who carried you. If your mother opted to put you up for adoption, you were still held in the arms of someone. You were here regardless of the choice your mother made, or that was made for her to give you up.

As you were experiencing the wonder and chaos of your birth, *you* opened your sensitive eyes and your sight was forced to acclimate to the brightness of light.

You *heard* voices, familiar and unfamiliar, and sounds you could not comprehend just yet. As the doctor, nurse or midwife swaddled you to keep you warm and placed you in your mother's arms or on her chest, you heard the familiar sound of her heartbeat, which made you feel at home as you also inherently knew your mother's *smell.*

This was your welcome to the world and the first awakening.

Reactions

In your awakening, you reacted to the stimuli that attacked your senses for the first time. The pain you felt, the cold air, the first breaths; they caused you to react by making your voice known as you began to cry. As in life, there are reactions to actions. When you reacted to the pain, your reaction caused a reaction from those who heard your voice. Their reaction to your action was that of joy and jubilation, not because they were happy you felt pain but because your cry was an indication that you were alive.

So it is, as you live and breathe throughout your seasons, there are times in life you have felt pain and your reaction to the pain begets a reaction from those surrounding you. The pain referenced isn't just physical; it can also be emotional, mental, psychological and even spiritual pain. As you experience pain, you ask questions like:

> "Why did you strike me?"
> "Why did you misrepresent me?"
> "Why did you say no to me?"
> "Why did you abandon me?"
> "Why was I rejected?"
> "Why did *I* accept that?"

The list can go on and on. Everything you experience in life is relational. From your first inhale to your last exhale, your actions, achievements, disappointments, trauma, pain, learning, triumphs, wins and losses have been connected to someone with whom you had a relationship and, many times, perfect strangers. In your first awakening, your primary caregiver held the greatest responsibility in your evolving, growing, nurturing… *becoming*. You were totally dependent on them. Your awakenings were many as you were becoming more conscious of every single thing your senses were experiencing.

Have you ever shared a pain point in your life with someone who can relate to your angst and they laughed or smiled as you bore your soul to them? And you wondered why they found your discomfort funny? Yes, there are people in this world that rejoice in seeing others hurt, but there are people near and dear to our hearts or those we look up to who find joy in seeing or knowing that growth is blossoming through our pain because they have experienced that pain and have grown and learned valuable life lessons as a result. They understand better than you that pain is essential for growth, evolution and the transformational process of you *be-coming*.

Symphonic Orchestration

You are here to live through many awakenings in this life.

The creation of You is likened to a symphony, which is composed of organs, cells and systems that are an orchestration fearfully and wonderfully created by God. Even if there are some anomalies within your making, somehow, you have survived and thrived. You did not succumb to a stigma but have defied every limitation you have been dealt. In this orchestration of the gift of you, perhaps in a musical sense, you were built in a minor chord.

I believe E minor is the most beautiful chord on the scale. It's dark yet beautiful with so many possibilities of movements and textures. A mosaic, if you will… broken pieces made into a beautiful work of art.

There are also chords within the orchestration of you that are augmented or diminished. Perhaps you exceed expectations in some areas and may even be a phenomenon, able to master complex tasks. That's the augmented chord. Perhaps it takes you a while to catch on to things, or, in the eyes of others, you lack certain qualities which diminishes your worth in their sight. That's the diminished chord. The most common of all the chords and keys is the major chord. Being a major chord or key is being normal without any anomalies, abnormalities or irregularities. All systems are functional and working in sync or in concert with each other.

In this orchestration, there is a nucleus without which you would resemble a ship without a sail under impending failure to survive. That nucleus is the heart... the beat of your drum is the tempo and syncopation of the song that is *You.* Anatomically, a normal heart rate ranges from 60 -100 beats per minute. Metaphorically, when it comes to the music of You, your orchestration can be measured as largo (40-60 bpm), larghetto (60-66 bpm), adagio (66-76 bpm), andante (76-108 bpm), moderato (108-120 bpm) allegro (120-168 bpm), presto (168-200 bpm), or prestissimo (>200 bpm). You may have been slow and easygoing, moderate, or off the charts and full throttle. The syncopation of the beat of your internal drum was the emphasis on any particular beat in your tempo. This was You to the core: How you were wired, your temperament.

Perhaps the orchestration of *You* is likened to jazz, an orchestration with complex harmonies, unlawful structures and movements, syncopated rhythms and a heavy emphasis on improvisation, meaning you make it up as you go. Some things that are easy to others are a conundrum to you and are beyond complex to you and you have to find a way to make what you have work.

The wonderful thing about jazz is that it is undefinable. Just when it's being understood and accepted, there's another change or movement that gets the attention of those who listen. Jazz is a mixture of many genres of music, and it makes you move or stand still attentively. Excuse the mixed metaphor, but I call it Jambalaya: Spicy, rambunctious, saucy and satiable or satisfying with the perfect roux. Jazz and music as a whole is a matter of taste and has many textures, colors and hues.

In the awakening, You were not the only one being awakened. You had an audience that began to witness the orchestration of you through their senses as well. *You* learned to teach them the tempo of the masterpiece of *You*. *You* were already giving lessons. They found out what you liked and what you didn't like. *You* taught them what was acceptable to your palate, who you liked or didn't like, what made you laugh and what made you cry. *You* taught them to love what they didn't like about you. *You* even began to learn how to manipulate them to get what you desired.

Everyday there is something you are becoming accustomed to: the smell of your mother's milk, the sounds and inflections of new voices, colors and shapes, recognizing faces and becoming familiar with each face you see, hunger, bodily discomfort, startling noises and the list goes on. You also are awakened to the power of your voice that when you cry, you get a lot of attention. When you smile, coo or laugh, you get high-pitched responses from those who surround you. All of these awakenings stimulate your continued growth. As your bones continue to grow and your muscles gain more strength, you begin to explore by sitting up independently, standing, scooting, crawling and then mastering the art of walking, running, falling down, skipping and eventually leaping.

For every awakening in life, it is necessary that you explore and find your key to life and the instrument you will play and live out loud in life. Know this, *you* are set apart and only *you* can fill that space in this symphony. You don't have to be the first, second or third chair… you just have to be in a chair and occupy your place in the major and minor orchestrations.

For every awakening, there is discovery in flexing your muscles and having a strong spine for sitting up, standing up and climbing up.

Here's the thing: you have to be "woke" to experience the awakenings in life.

What are you doing in this season of your life to stay woke or to see the possibilities that are awaiting your awakening? What are you doing to recalibrate so that you can accelerate? The world is your oyster. You have already proven what you're made of; afterall, you have already passed through the eye of the needle, if you will and survived to tell the story.

Total Dependency

In this season of your awakening, you were totally dependent on your caregivers. You would not have survived without them. Care may be subjective in this case as you may have not been given proper care, yet, you're still here. This means *You* adjusted and survived in spite of the injustice of your caregiver or the lack of resources they had to give you the absolute best. You were not physically, mentally or psychologically able to provide the basic necessities of life for yourself.

Your growth in every area of life—biological, psychological, social and spiritual—was dependent on food, hygiene, affection, nurture and your senses being stimulated through communication. Without these, your demise would have been imminent.

Today, more than likely, you cannot remember how you were cared for. If there are any references, they are from stories you have been told. Suffice it to say that your growth depended on someone, and then *you* ingested, digested, obtained knowledge, received instruction, adapted, experienced, learned and endured.

Your tiny little brain was on cerebral overload and *you* mastered this crash course of growth and learning.

On the **Surface**, you were just a little child, needy and totally dependent. ***Deep***... You were a wondrous creation with potential, a purpose and endless possibilities.

Development

Up to this point in life, *you* have been busy, seemingly doing nothing. However, *You* have done exploits and have experienced many wins. *You* are fearfully and wonderfully made, and the possibilities for you to leave a lasting legacy are endless.

The emphasis on *You* in each season is meant to awaken your consciousness on your process of becoming and your tenacity to win from the very beginning. There are numerous rebirths as you continue in life and encounter its ebbs and flows. It behooves you to recognize that for every rebirth and every season in life, you've already overcome obstacles, learned lessons and established your aptitude and ability to win.

Development is imperative for the best outcome.

Environment

In this season of development, *you* continued to consume everything your eyes were seeing, ears were hearing, tongue tasted, nose smelled, skin felt and heart received. Your learning was more in-depth than when you were in your infantile stage. Throughout the childhood stage, you were learning the complexities of life and your innate instinct was to survive because *you* were going somewhere.

As it was then, so it is even today: Your evolution continues. And if you are to thrive and grow, it is necessary to be in the right environment in this season and in every season to come.

The right environment is essential for your development. In order for developmental growth in every area of life to be optimal, the environment must be favorable, productive, beneficial and, above all, non-poisonous. The atmosphere of your surroundings will determine the viability of your growth. This includes your physical, mental, emotional, psychological and spiritual wellness. Even today, as we hear about and witness the environmental changes, we see the effect of climate change worldwide. Damage has been done and has affected the very air we breathe because of toxicity in the atmosphere.

The environment we lived in and those who surrounded us had a major impact on the influence we would bring into the world.

Among the issues we face in life, there is one common denominator: relationships. Everything is relational. Our development is predicated on our surroundings, whose space we're in and who's in our space. Our strengths are affirmed or rejected. Our weaknesses are co-signed or challenged. We adopt strong and positive character as well as our fears, -isms, schisms and all of our dirty laundry, baggage and trash.

The people who have crossed our paths, immediate family members, extended family, educators, people who have come into our lives for brief encounters, pastors, classmates, coworkers, employers and the like, help shape us into who we are. It is usually those who are closest to us that have the most significant impact on our lives—positive or negative.

Humble Beginnings

I was born with a blank slate. My fond recollections consist of apartment 401 in the Ickes on 24th and State Street in Chicago. Life was simple—there were no cares in the world as far as I knew. Roaches were normal to me. I grew up in a two-parent family, and as the youngest of three, I soaked up everything my senses could feed me. I wasn't aware that I was learning.

I knew very little but took in everything my eyes beheld; my mother going to work every morning and my father going to work every afternoon; my two older sisters leaving to go to school; going to church every Tuesday, Friday, Saturday and *all* day Sunday as a family; my mother and father having a healthy, loving relationship.

I heard everything my ears received–news and mystery theater on WBBM radio, stories that captured my imagination, Gospel music and sound recordings by Sam Cooke, Clara Ward, James Cleveland, Albertina Walker and the Caravans and the Roberta Martin Singers are the ones I remember hearing the most in my younger years (we only listened to Gospel music). I also remember the music of Motown that my siblings would sneak and listen to when our parents were not home, conversations between my mother and father, telephone and in-person conversations between adults, conversations between my older sisters and their friends, preached messages at church and the melodic music my father made on the guitar as well as from choirs and soloists.

I devoured everything I was fed through my mouth–soul food, fried chicken, mashed potatoes, cornbread dressing, macaroni and cheese, smothered cubed steak and pork chops, homemade biscuits with butter and molasses, cornbread and buttermilk, just to name a few.

Every odor I smelled identified a person, place or thing–the smell of the food that tickled my olfactory system and caused me to anticipate the impending feast that would satiate my taste buds and hunger; the smell of Old Spice after shave that my dad would wear at bedtime and after a bath; the odors that were offensive and caused me to frown and step away from the source, such as the smell of the school or the smell of urine or vomit on the L train.

I felt everything that touched me physically and emotionally. Many things I felt physically were attached to an emotion. The cold and blustery wind on my face and legs as we waited for the bus and train during winter was very uncomfortable. The sting of the extension cord on my skin when I got a whipping as a punishment for every infarction left me frightened, unhappy and very much in pain.

These are just a few of the faint memories that formed and shaped the mosaic of my recollections and most distant memories. These recollections are the things that stood out to me and had the most profound effect on my growth, thereby becoming my foundation.

Nature Vs. Nurture

You were born with personality and character traits that you naturally introduced to everyone in your new world. Your nature was already embedded in the fabric of your life. You may have been strong-willed and vocal or soft-spoken and docile. When placed in the environment of your family, there may have been a tug of war in this stage of development called nature vs. nurture. The nucleus or core of your existence was certainly challenged by their treatment, response to and interaction with you. If they recognized your predisposition and nurtured and cared for you with love and adoration, you should have had a well-served and balanced life. But if you were nurtured in a way that would reject, challenge and punish you, that could impact your development.

You were organic soil, having all the nutrients needed to grow and be sustainable to produce viable seed and fruit that would yield even more of your essence to ensure a legacy with your DNA. Cultivation, feeding, watering and replenishing from those who planted you were necessary for optimal results in your evolution.

Growth

As a child, eating or ingesting everything in your environment caused you to grow physically, psychologically, socially and spiritually. Your diet for growth comprised learning, understanding, eating, digesting and excreting.

> *The only way not to grow is not to be fed.*

As a co-owner of a mortuary, I know full well what the end of growth looks like and it behooves us to awaken our perspective on life, recognizing that only living things and people grow.

It is necessary to understand that your evolution is the manifestation and is essential for growth. From conception to birth or seed to infancy, there was change and growth. A seed was planted in an earthen vessel and it had your name on it. From the moment that seed was planted, *YOU* innately began to evolve. There was a process for you to come forth and be presented to the world, and in the fullness of time, *YOU* emerged and that cycle of change and growth has continued to this day. Now, right now, *you* are living in the middle of that cycle, and intentionally or unintentionally, growth is taking place whether you are in the ideal environment for it or not.

Some years ago, I had a plant called the Mother in Law's tongue. I loved plants, but I couldn't be bothered, so I had cacti plants and Mother in Law's tongue plants, as they required little care and were hard to kill.

This Mother in Law's tongue was in the living room and I watered it just enough to keep it from dying. I was amazed it lived so long. At the time I was living in a split-level townhome, and this plant was on another level in the living room that no one went in unless they needed to vacuum and dust. This poor plant would have grown at a much faster pace had I watered it more and maybe put it in a larger pot.

I later acquired two parakeets, Pete and RePeat. Their cage was in the corner of the kitchen and I soon realized I had a problem. Food and feathers did not go together, so I had my son take the birds upstairs into the living room. After a while, I began to notice a smell when I walked into my home. I could not identify what the scent was and where it came from. But because it wasn't alarming to my senses, I assumed it was a fragrant lotion or bath and body product and didn't look into it any further. After coming home several times and noticing the smell was stronger, I decided to investigate. I followed my sense of smell to the next level to identify and satisfy my curiosity. Lo and behold, the unattended plant had bloomed full and healthy white blossoms.

That plant was in a conducive environment for growth. It received proper sunlight every day, but it was not nurtured, properly cared for, paid attention to and was undergrown for its age because the pot it was in was too small for the roots to go deeper and the stalks to grow taller. After Pete and RePeat were placed in close proximity to the plant, it woke up and became productive in a different way. In spite of the lack of care and stunted growth, this living thing blossomed and bore fruit. When the birds were placed in the living room, the plant began to respond to the bird's song.

Reflect on your life in the second season of development. Was your environment conducive for growth? Were you well nurtured and nourished? Were the people in your proximity the catalyst to a healthy and wealthy life? There was something you knew that you were not taught that caused you to pivot to survive and not die. *You* innately continued to adapt to things, people and situations that were beyond your control. *You* compensated for any lack or limitations by finding a way to survive and thrive. *You* continued to breathe!

Arrested Development

As with the plant, perhaps your development has been detained and held in contempt. Maybe there was a growth deficiency due to your adoption of malignant thinking and mindset based on what you ingested and digested or what you were not fed by those whose care you were in. Your mind was set, sealed and conditioned to limited and elementary thinking.

Physiologically and anatomically, growth happened. However, without change to your environment, you were left malnourished mentally, emotionally, spiritually and psychologically.

On the **Surface,** you are an adult. So the perception and expectation of others are that you have the full package. However, when you speak, what you partake in, or even your body language reveals what you have or have not experienced in your youthful developmental stage.

I'm sure you've encountered adults who've whined or have become combative and had a tantrum when things didn't go their way. Their mindset and actions didn't match their age. At some point, their minds became arrested developmentally. When life gets uncomfortable or when given the opportunity for growth, these individuals push back, complain, fight, run away, deny or bargain instead of yielding to the process of adaptation. If this person is you and there are one or many deficiencies you can identify in your stage of development (and I believe we all have a few), can you dig **deep** and find the MOXIE (grit, courage and determination) with the great expectation of adopting the bigger, better, BOLDER, accomplished You?

As you go **Deep** beneath the surface, *You* still have the fortitude you had at the beginning of the evolution of *You* to meet the challenge and take action by:

- Arresting your current mindset
- Being intentional
- Developing mental clarity

- Adopting new ideals
- Aborting mental instability
- Changing your current environment

If you feel stuck, trapped or that you're a product of your environment and your growth is stunted, is it possible that you can get in proximity to a catalyst for growth?

Growth is critical for us all—and where there's no growth, there's stagnation, retardation, failure to thrive and death.

Your second stage of development was most crucial because it was the stage for learning and you becoming who you currently are. At this very moment, you are not the sum total of what or who you will be or are meant to be. This sense of self-identity is incumbent on *you* to be vulnerable, as you were when you were totally dependent on the guardians of your life. They saw you and knew you from a surface or superficial level and maybe just beneath the surface; however, you have continued to evolve. And just as your guardians became accustomed to you as you were, *You* have the responsibility to tap into yourself on a much deeper level.

Your personal growth, professional growth and leadership growth require striving for more, for better. You have developed well based on your experiences growing with what you've had to work with. But you know there is more. You recognize you are not complete. You desire to satiate your thirst and tap into your full potential. Or are you ok with just being ok? Are you really ok? Is ok good enough? Are you ok settling for less, or are you accepting what is unacceptable if you are to have an exceptional life? Can you see yourself beneath the surface better than ok, fulfilled and joyous as you evolve?

Investigate your environment, humble beginnings and growth in your developmental stage to identify the points in your life during which your development was arrested.

On the **Surface**, how did you perceive your world? **Deep** under the surface, how did your youthful experiences serve you?

Birthings of Thought

IMAGERY

Seeing through a glass darkly... and then, Face to Face

THE MIRROR depicted in the photo is merely an object of the reflection of a likeness of a person, place or thing. Mirror is a noun that reflects a noun. It can be utilized as a simple decoration on a wall, standing in a corner, on a counter or in a person's hand. The undeniable property of a mirror is that any object that is in its path will be reflected. The mirror has a purpose.

A mirror is a noun that reflects a noun.

After having a devastating encounter with someone who held a massive chunk of my heart, I was overwhelmed, depressed, rejected, left feeling powerless and defeated. To me, this event triggered my emotions and affirmed what I was told about my worth as a child. It was as if the tattoos etched in my psyche were refreshed and reinforced. I went into the bathroom so that my children wouldn't see me so distraught. I closed the door and sat on the "throne," if you will. I did not want to feel anymore. I did not want to live anymore. I wanted my heart to get a rest from beating so fast, so hard—or at all. I couldn't imagine getting any lower in spirit. Words to pray escaped me as if I never knew how. However, I did remember to say, "JESUS!" I screamed His name in silence. That name, JESUS, was my SOS call for relief. I was despondent and, simply put, tore up from the floor. As I sat there, I cried so hard, it felt like the lobes of my brain were being stretched apart from the back of my head. After a few minutes of what felt like a descent into insanity, God spoke into my spirit and said, "Get up! Look in the mirror." Mind you; this was one of the ugliest cries in my life to that date. I got up and I looked in the mirror. What I beheld almost took me out. I didn't know what was worse: the conundrum I was in that had me spiraling or what I saw in the mirror. It wasn't pretty. It was then that God began to speak to me.

God: What do you see?

Me: I'm ugly. I'm worthless; I am good for nothing. I am a failure. My nose is flat. I'm fat. I look like a monkey.

Now, I can laugh at those thoughts. Then, they were very much ingrained into my brain.

My face was oozing tears and other bodily fluids from my nose. On the **surface**, I looked like a hot mess.

I believe it was by divine intervention that I turned on the hot water, let it get as hot as I could stand it, immersed a clean towel, squeezed it, put it to my face and took a long, deep breath. The dialogue continued after I cleaned my face and beheld my red, puffy eyes.

God: Now, look again; what do you see?

Me: (Soberly and unapologetically) *I Am* a woman after God's heart; I have a good heart, pure and holy for His glory. *I Am* fearfully and wonderfully made. *I Am* a winner. *I Am* more than a conqueror. *I Am* a beautiful soul from the inside out. *I Am* an overcomer. *I Am* the head, not the tail. *I Am* a jewel in His crown.

This defining mirror moment became what I eventually began to call IMAGERY:

A reflection of what is seen through a lens or a mirror. Even though I couldn't pray just moments before that first IMAGERY moment, the affirmation that happened in the mirror and the conversation that God had with me and through me was so astounding I couldn't focus on what had me in a knot.

Before this, I had never paid attention to what or who I saw in the mirror because my perception of myself was what I was told in my developmental stage. I emphatically believed I was ugly, would never accomplish anything, that I was good for nothing and nobody, that I did not matter, that I was dumb and stupid all at the same time. Everything I had ingested was negative. I had settled for a defeatist mindset and attitude because of all of the no's in life I had been dealt. As a result, I stopped asking because *no*, *can't* and *ain't* had become my portion. These developmental hiccups stunted my growth on so many levels. I was insecure and defined myself based on my personal connections. I was somebody's wife, Andrae and Nikki's mother, a daughter-in-law and a member of the church I attended. Period. End of story.

As I reflect on this IMAGERY experience and encounter with myself, I remember how I felt. The heaviness was lifted and I felt much lighter. The inhale and exhale I had taken into the hot towel revealed life to me. I felt good about myself because I knew the words I had spoken to myself the second time were spoken from my heart. My core comprised noble and affirming attributes that added value to my character… my *Be*ing. For the first time in my life, I believed that I had a voice and that I was worth speaking life into myself and listening to myself. Why? Because I knew I could trust myself to be honest.

This was the first of many Imagery or mirror moments. I would soon forget to remember what I saw when the vicissitudes of life would arrest my mind as I would focus on the problems and not seek solutions. You see, my mind had been set for defeat. The tattoos of self-doubt in my psyche were inked in hues of dark colors and negativity.

Two decades would pass before I had these mirror moments on a regular basis. If you were a fly on the wall and were related to me, you probably would have looked into having me committed to a mental institution because I was talking to myself, asking questions and answering. These IMAGERY moments saved my life, changed my life, kept me mentally sane and sound because I realized that God would speak to me and through me.

IMAGERY is using the "Mirror" as a catalyst for self-reflection, self-awareness, self-inflection, self-honesty and the *conception* of *you Be*coming the born-again You.

It is imperative that you are committed to *You* while doing the IMAGERY exercises, as this is not for the faint of heart. Life is not for the faint of heart… It's for the faint, ready to wake up! This is an opportunity for an intentional awakening.

Along this journey of *be*coming, you will get to know you from the surface to a much deeper level. Your journey is a process so buckle up... because your destination will land you in a place at the four clover intersections of

Surrender, Confidence, Potential and Purpose! At this point, you will be able to stand in the mirror, naked and not ashamed.

Be*Come… Come to Be… Show up to *Be

Double Take

When looking through the lenses of your eyes into the mirror, literally or reflectively, at first sight, you only see the superficial. You see the ***surface***. You only see the outermost layer: your skin, which is covering something that is deeper than the surface.

The skin you're in can be likened to the outer layer of an onion. It covers and protects your vital organs and systems that lie beneath the surface. The first take of what you see in the mirror may or may not look appealing to you depending on your perception, perspective and point of view. Skin is the largest organ of your body, which itself is made of layers. The top outermost layer of skin is made of dead cells that sheds and regenerates itself, peels, flakes, absorbs, regulates your temperature, and, above all, protects your entire body. The skin you're in is not the same skin you were born in; however, it has the same properties and the same DNA. So, why don't the same possibilities and potential you were born with not apply to you today? The skin you were born in has regenerated as you have grown, absorbing so much from the elements in life and everything you have exposed it to externally, as well as what you have ingested from food, skin care products, inhaled from your environment, as well as stress.

On the ***surface***, what you see in the mirror may be thick, thin, supple, tight, smooth, rough, resilient, oily, dry, or brittle. Whatever the category your skin falls under, it is necessary that you treat it accordingly. Looking in the mirror requires you to see and identify what is dead on the surface and exfoliate it, so that you can live as a human, ***be***ing everything you, from the beginning, were called to ***be***. Do you really see what you see?

As you speak, what you see in the second take requires corrective lenses that change your perspective as you gain clarity. ***Deep*** within, you're so much more than what you see on the surface. Everything ***deep*** within you is living, operating and functioning at a reasonable capacity. ***Deep*** within you, *You* know more than you know. *You* know about *you*. **Deep** within you lies your character, personality, spirit and soul, all of which may need some pruning, debridement and grafting. Buried ***deep*** within you are seeds to be released and planted to bring forth fruit. The question you must answer is, will you produce good fruit or strange fruit? The only way to get the best outcome is for you to identify your now mindset so that *you* can rewire, rewrite and reframe your story in *your* book of life.

It is imperative that you weigh the words you speak of yourself. After all, *you* live in *you*. The narrative and actions of others who come into your life for whatever reason, however long of a season and/or for a lifetime, can make you, break you, or cause you to be stangnant and retard your growth.

I must interject this disclaimer: As a Christian, I believe that we all are here because we were a thought in the mind of God and have a purpose. Even though this book's subtitle is "The Evolution of *You*," evolution is not a reference to that of transitioning from an ape into a human. If you don't believe in God, then you can recalibrate that to your liking or perspective. Whatever you believe is your prerogative and your truth. My voice speaks my truth unapologetically, respectfully and non-combatively that in the fullness of time at the perfect time, we became the evidence of a thought in the mind of God for a reason, a purpose, a season and in this lifetime. We were not just thought of to merely exist. We were a thought to be made manifest in this world so that we could show up and show out, to walk in and on purpose intentionally, unapologetically, seriously and fiercely with confidence in who we are, why we're here and striving to hold our ground from the foundation from which we were called and on which we are planted.

Knowing who you are from the inside out through God's eyes is imperative to your success and significance in life. There was a poignant lesson in this experience, some of which I want to share with you:

When the cares of life get you down and you feel defeated in your spirit... Get UP!!!!

When you get up... Step Forward.

When you look in the mirror... Be honest.

When you look in the mirror... Say what God sees.

Begin to take on the character of God: Loving, kind, holy, just, faithful, merciful, forgiving, gracious, patient, slow to anger, powerful, just to name a few.

Begin to take on the mind of God.

Begin to speak the word of God concerning you.

Release the healing power of God in your own life and stop waiting for a feel-good affirmation from someone else.

Stop waiting for an apology from someone who grossly offended you and will never offer one.

FORGIVE.

Prophetically speak into your own life the unadulterated word and will of God.

Tell on yourself, to yourself and to God. Don't make excuses for your mess.

Expose *you* to *You*. Admit and quit the things in your life that weigh you down and keep you from being the awesome being *You* are.

Get your earthly house clean so that God's divine nature can saturate you and you can walk in the fullness of His power.

Discipline is Key

"This is just who I Am" is not allowed until you *know* who you are. Don't get it twisted, because as you find your wonderful self and reclaim who you are at the nucleus or core of you, your attitude will determine your altitude.

Who you have become is not (or may not be) who you are! You are still evolving to *Be*-come. Life is a process and no one living has arrived. We are constantly evolving, transforming and transitioning, and the process isn't easy. You are so much more powerful than you realize. God loves you and has invested in you the power to be whole.

I Am… I See

I am the first student of IMAGERY and I continue to learn and grow as a result of it. I choose to be nothing less than transparent with this because I'm a seed sower and I don't know anyone else who has had Imagery moments in this precise manner. 38 years ago, the beginning of this chapter began; that was my first take. Here is a more recent take that I am sharing with you now through corrective lenses. Exponential growth has taken place in my life and I am still growing. Remember, as you look in the mirror, the question is: "What do you see?"

What *I See*

I SEE brown skin un-taut.

The lenses through which I initially see don't penetrate the ***surface.***

I see through the lenses of my once slanted eyes. With age, stresses, distresses, tragedies, disappointments, failures, brokenness, war wounds, disillusions, worries, depression, the elements of the atmosphere I breathe and the cares of this life, gravity has worked against my facial features.

Yet, ***Deep*** beneath the surface of the external…

I SEE beauty within (with & in) through corrective lenses. Because I see through the glass (mirror) darkly, I have opted for and chosen elective or optional corrective surgery (medically, you would call it cataract removal… (I call it taking the blinders off) so that I may see with clearer vision.

As I behold, I SEE Beauty ***deeper*** than skin.
I SEE with discernment, the image of I Am (my Father) in me.
I SEE that *I AM* Perfectly Imperfect
I SEE that my Flaws make me unique.
I SEE that my failures have set me up for success.

I SEE that the negativities and hardships in life have toughened the skin I'm in.
I SEE that in spite of my fears, my faith has brought wholeness and has been my portion.
I SEE gold wedged within the cracks of my brokenness and welded by the fire that has cured me, a broken vessel, the potter's masterpiece.
I SEE VISION!
I SEE Women, just like me being lifted, transformed, minds being reset, renewed, restored, rejuvenated and empowered to walk in their wealthy place, Spirit, Soul and Body; whole, complete and entire.
I SEE ***promise, potential, purpose, destiny, trials, tragedy, triumph.***

C'est Qui Je Suis:
This is who I Am

I AM my Father's daughter.
I AM a courier of His DNA.
I AM predestined.
I AM a choice.
I AM a promise.
I AM a possibility.
I AM a great big bundle of potentiality.
I AM Love, I AM Spirit, I AM Life, I AM Hope,
I AM Faith.
I AM flawlessly flawed.

I AM strong, yet fragile.
I AM scarred with war wounds of this life... Yet,
I AM healed
I AM a visionary.
I AM the express Image *{Reflection}* of "I AM" in me
I AM worth it!

WHO do you say *You Are?*
I challenge you to have an IMAGERY moment!!!
Unleash *your* poetic voice
Look in the Mirror. What do you see?

I'm Worth It

I'm worth it because of the hefty price I have paid time and time again, not just in finances but the price of pouring out of myself into someone else's birthing.

I'm worth it because of the seeds planted, the incubation, the gestation and the pain in birthing.

I'm worth it because I've learned from my failures.

I'm worth it because God said I'm worth it.

I'm worth it because I have been allowed to laugh in the face of danger.

God says I'm worth it and has set a table before me to sit in the presence of my enemies,

I'm worth it because I've overcome and defied limits and thrived in spite of tears, depression, rejection, tragedy and self-loathing… I'm still standing!

I'm worth it because of the goodness I've allowed to ooze out of me to bless others and to invoke change through my pain.

I'm worth dressing up and liking what I see.

I'm worth looking in the mirror and beholding beauty.

I'm worth winking at myself and saying, "and God said: That's good."

I'm worth it because I have an inheritance. I am my father's daughter.

Now, Go to that quiet place and have an "IMAGERY" moment. Look in the Mirror and be a voyeur in your own life. This is a place of reflection, a place to look introspectively, a place of resolve, honesty, redemption, consecration, rededication, restoration, revival, a place of absolution, empowerment and healing.

I pray that this moment of transparency will serve as a catalyst to the evolution of You personified.

Birthings of Thought

Season 3

The Abyss

At this point in your evolution, you have gone through many seasons. The season of "The Abyss" is a time of figuring things out about you as an individual away from the noise. This is where the rubber meets the road. This is a season of reckoning and reconstruction. In this season, *You* have evolved, developed and mirrored what you've ingested, absorbed, accepted and rejected. You remember what you've learned and experienced from others and the world you live in. There are ideals, ideologies and beliefs that have been etched into your psyche, some good and some bad. You are searching for answers because you are at the precipice of being on your own and charting your own course.

The Abyss is dark and daunting. It is seemingly a place of your undoing and imminent demise. The comfort of dependency is over, and if you are going to beautifully evolve, you must go through this grueling process of transformation. The cost of your transformation is expensive and you will have to determine if you're worth investing in being the best version of yourself.

Yes, there are many versions of you:

The ***You*** whose character and personality was set at birth is the fingerprint that sets you apart and is not duplicable.

The ***You*** that adopted and mirrored everything you learned and experienced.

The ***You*** that ***You*** believe others expect you or want you to be.

Haven't you been here before in the beginning when you were just a seed and raced to the egg, through the fallopian tube to the womb? Yes, *You* did that and stayed through the process. You evolved and developed through nature and nurture. Now you're repeating the process of being in the womb, only it's different this time. You're conscious and this place is not as comfortable as being in your mother's womb. However, even though you're in the dark and you're finding your footing and direction, the Abyss is also a place of safety. A protective covering that provides safety and shelter from the harsh elements. Winds that can blow you away, storms of life that can wash you away and heat from the sun that can dry you up and drain all your strength.

We go through life after we've been nurtured (or not). After our minds and bodies have been developed and we've gleaned from all of the stimuli from our parents, relatives, our friends and from society, we all experience situations that push us to *Be*come who we are as individuals. More often than not, we come to a fork in the road or hit a bump that requires us to do a self-evaluation. We realize that some of those things we have learned are not serving us well. We realize that some of the things we were exposed to didn't serve us well. We realize we have become morbidly obese (not just physically) because we absorbed and ate unhealthy things that are detrimental to our bodies, to our spirits and ultimately could destroy our very souls. There are many things imparted into us that were and are lovely, pure, true, good and of virtue that we rebelled against and rejected.

Slipping into Darkness

At this point, we must steal away from all of those things that are not good for us. Some of those things are good *to* us because that's what we've come to know and understand; however, what's good to us isn't always good for us. We are still evolving to ***be***come what and who we are to the core, the season we've been looking forward to. Did you ever say, "I can't wait to be grown and on my own, do what I want to do, when I want to do it and with whom I want to do it?" I did. Initially, you are in preparation for this season. You made plans and prepared yourself for adulthood in anticipation of executing and living your life out loud.

Like a caterpillar, you have eaten and grown, and you are now spinning the fabric of your life into an abyss that literally is hanging by a thread. Your own essence (thoughts, ideas, aspirations, culture, character, beliefs, mindset) is what you start with and then hang from. You continue spinning until you've spun yourself into a thick, hard encasement where you are stuck and seemingly there is no way out.

Legally and chronologically you may be an adult, however you won't really be a bonafide grown-up adult until after you've gone into the Abyss and culminated this season. Your process of *be*coming is spun out of you. You have made this tough shell or built a fortified wall that will withstand the storms and protect you from the elements. Your walls are not made of mire for you are clothed in what was always in you. You are very protective of your space.

The Abyss is very uncomfortable. It is thick and insulated so that nothing or no one can penetrate it. It does not reveal what's inside at all. You are truly the definition of a closet phenomenon. It is almost like a prison; however, there are no bars, you are surrounded by a continuous fortified wall with no doors. This is solitary confinement.

As a caterpillar eats and experiences exponential growth, for continued growth to take place, it bursts out of its skin and eats the old skin as it has vital nutrients it needs for the sustainability of the journey ahead.

It's dark and a wet mess, but *you* are ***be***coming a beautiful *you*. Everything you need for sustenance is already in you. You will not die of starvation and you will not perish from over-exposure. You are resilient and will use what you have in you to make it through this transition. Death seems to be imminent, but you will find the strength to survive and thrive. You may long to get out, but you know this stage is necessary for the journey ahead. It may even seem that the walls are closing in on you and then you realize while in this dark place that true transformation is taking place. While you are seemingly disintegrating, some of what you are shedding is forming into wings. The excess weight and baggage are being utilized in your favor to be liberated and free to soar. The truth is: Nothing we learn in life is unnecessary. It's those unnecessary things that we go through that help us to be who God has called us to be.

Withdrawn Into Privacy

I was in the Abyss for a long time. Ten years. On my own for the first time in my life, transitioning, getting to know me, not being defined by someone else or who I was connected to, establishing my own identity. I was reaching within myself and trusting no one. I shut all the other voices and noises out and became willing to change my perspective through corrective lenses by taking the blinders off. I allowed the creator to circumcise my ears so that I could directly hear only His voice. I chose to shut myself into my home, which was what I called my safe place, because I knew it was necessary for my new beginning and for mental and spiritual stability.

This was a pivotal point in my life as I was clinically depressed. I had attempted to end my life because breathing was too exhausting and I had no compass for the next course of my life. I was unsuccessful at attempting to cross the line to be God in my own life by having the audacity to dictate that I would die.

To document my state of mind, I wrote one-liners in a journal to express my angst: "Drowning, Yet breathing."

"Damaged Goods"

"Breathing without a Heartbeat"

The essence of who "I Am" had not yet been revealed to me because I was in the Abyss. It was dark, with no light in sight. So, in essence, I was double insulated.

At this point in my life, I should have been coming out of the Abyss, but life threw a curveball. At the age of 43, I began living alone for the first time ever. I had always been dependent, co-dependent and had my children who were dependent on me. Now, I was separated and then divorced, a statistic I had never imagined I would be in. Six months after my new single status was declared and sealed, tragedy struck again. This was not a curveball. I was blindsided: I lost my daughter.

It was the thickest kind of darkness with no light in sight. I pondered how anyone could recover from this.

Withdrawing from the elements of the world was the best way for me to attempt to secure my footing and to not succumb to any additional unnecessary pain. Even in this place of uncertainty, there were some things I had that worked in my favor.

I had a cemented spiritual foundation.This is where God and I met face to face, 1 on 1, as it was necessary for me to withdraw from church, the organized part of religion which is frowned upon. In order for me to survive this present darkness, my gaze had to be on my creator, not the creature (the preacher). I must admit, I became spoiled because, even though I was in a very dark place, His light made all things palatable. I would not be writing this book had I not withdrawn. For me, this was IMAGERY University!

My innate fortitude was still intact (even though I didn't realize I had been operating in my essence from **deep** to **surface**) the true essence of who I Am.

The second thing I had going for me was that I was taught to take no for an answer, so I was familiar with being stuck and adapting to situational and mental darkness. In my development stage, I had learned to accept the things I could not change.

The Abyss is not for punks. Those who refuse to put on their corrective lenses will never emerge from the Abyss because they refuse to see the light. These are those who are determined to occupy space frivolously without regard for what it takes to be significant in this world. These are those who absorb the atmosphere and attempt to suck the life out of those who try to lift them. They are takers, not givers, and partake at the table of bad influencers. Also, the faint of heart will only emerge when they decide they are willing to be a part of their own process, want change, are willing to be an active participant in their own transformation and are ready to see the light and wake up.

Life… is not for the faint of heart
It's for the faint, ready to wake up!

Randy Newman wrote the lyrics to a song that became the theme song for the TV show *Monk*.

It's a Jungle out There
It's a jungle out there
Disorder and confusion everywhere
No one seems to care
Well I do
Hey, who's in charge here?
It's a jungle out there
Poison in the very air we breathe
Do you know what's in the water that you drink?

Well, I do, and it's amazing
People think I'm crazy 'cause I worry all the time
If you paid attention, you'd be worried too
You better pay attention
Or this world we love so much might just kill you
I could be wrong now, but I don't think so
'Cause there's a jungle out there
It's a jungle out there

Again, this is when the world is your oyster. From a growth and development perspective, chronologically you graduate from high school (or not), go to college or trade school (or not), get a job and start a career, fall in love (or lust), get married (or shop around), become a mom or dad, get your own apartment or purchase your first home, have sole responsibility for your life, how you will finance life as well as how you will deal with the consequences of your choices as an adult. This can be a dark place because there are so many variables, so many unknowns.

In this season, matters of the heart are the things that are defined, pruned, debrided, tested and proven.

Perception, Perspective, Point of View

The most amazing thing is that as you hung on to the spun silk that is a part of your essence and you continued to become, that hard shell or wall began to disintegrate. From the ***deep***est part of your being, your perception, perspective and point of view began to take on new meaning. You began to question what you've seen, heard, felt and tasted. You rationalized the meaning of all of the things you've ingested and have become an intricate part of your life up until this moment. You investigate how these things have served you in a positive way. You begin to regurgitate the things that leave a nasty taste in your mouth and things that used to be funny in your youthful folly are not funny anymore.

As you investigate, you take names of people, places, things and life events that brought you to the beliefs you have ascribed to, and again, question if they are based on opinions, theories, rhetoric, or truth. You search for answers to gain absolution and resolve your quandary. You begin to realize that your reality is more than what you see on the ***surface*** or what you feel… it's what you know at a much ***deeper*** level. You notice that the orchestration and music of your life have expanded and nursery rhymes no longer satiate your sense of wellbeing. They are simply a reminder of what was and the music of your life begins to reflect more complex stanzas, chords, rhythms, textures and styles in the composition of your life.

During this time of reflection or Imagery moments, you honestly examine and confront your infarctions and sins of your past; things about you that weigh you down and keep you from excelling. Things like identifying the difference between laziness and lack of motivation, examining the difference between humility and cowardliness, lawfulness or principle, promiscuity or free-spirited insanity, lying or exaggeration, over sensitivity, an angry disposition and calling out ideologies you deeply know are unsavory. And you've accepted them as ok because you've become accustomed to reveling in your acts of indiscretion and blowing it off by saying "that's just who I Am."

Investigation, examination, identification and exposure are the key to absolute transformation. It takes Moxie to face these things that hinder you from truly living out loud wholly, fiercely and unapologetically. Truthfully identifying your infarctions and exposing them to yourself allows you to investigate the root of the fruit, and only when you face these truths can you liberate yourself to *Be* the authentic *you* from ***Deep*** to ***Surface***. Facing your fears and recognizing fear as False Evidence Appearing Real and a bluff or bully. On the surface, what you fear is insurmountable, but deep fear has no teeth. If you say it until you believe it, you will overcome it.

On the surface what you fear is insurmountable, but, deep, fear has no teeth.

Maturity is taking place and a wonderful change is happening. In time you will not look like what you look like now. As your hard shell thins, it becomes transparent and you finally begin to see a glimmer of light, and this light gets brighter as time goes by. You have a new point of view. What you now see while looking outward from within is so much clearer and with a different vantage point of view. You are at the dawn of a new day, new chapter, new season. Oh my, all things new, again? Yes! You've done this before. The moment you emerged into this world in your beginning and now, here you are again, upside down and poised to emerge again into a new season. Hang in there! The process in this season of the Abyss is almost over. It's ok to wait for the fullness of time so that you will be ready to fly. Premature emergence can cause you to be grounded indefinitely and you were created to soar.

Two Opposing Forces

As sure as you're reading this book, there is a negative force that is formed against you to keep you from reaching your expected end.

Any opposing force, be it limiting beliefs, hindering mindsets, or imprints seared in your psyche, must be met with equal or more powerful resistance so that you can release the manifestation of success, influence and significance.

Growing up in Chicago in a very religious and limiting environment informed my experiences as an adult. By the time I'd become older, all I knew were limitations, not possibilities. "No" was my opposing force. If I was told "no," I wouldn't persist. I wouldn't even ask. A thought or idea was just a thought or idea. "No" was the action. I didn't allow myself to dream. To me, I was only defined by whom I was connected to, and my name was the relationship to whom I was connected. It would take 40 years for me to realize that in spite of what I thought of myself or how I saw myself, I had been opposing the forces of "no" all along. The problem was the normality of my mindset kept me limited. My opposition was passive and unintentional. What made me resist was my CORE, intuition and the people I served. I learned that resistance to limitations is the driving force to success, influence and significance. I accepted average and mediocrity, but there was a resistance within me that was never satisfied with the status quo.

> ***Resistance to limitations is the driving force to success.***

Life is like a card game. There's the dealer and there are the players. The objective is to win and the adulation of a win is sweet! All games are not created equal. You may be dealt one card, and as the game progresses, pull from the deck, not knowing the value of the card you will pull. You may be dealt several cards with different values and must strategize which cards to put on the table to ensure a win. Sometimes you get a good hand and sometimes you get a crappy hand. Sometimes you pull a winning card from the deck, and sometimes, the value of the card you pull doesn't have enough value. In our personal and professional lives, we decide if we are the dealer who owns the house and the deck or the player hoping and wishing for a win. Some of us are the players who depend on the luck of the draw and must deal with whatever the outcome is.

There was a hand dealt to you and there have been stories told to you that were not true or misconstrued. You believed them, which gave you a certain perspective and belief system. There have been things you've witnessed through your senses. You've seen, you've heard, you've felt or touched, you've smelled, you've tasted. Whatever you've ingested, you became those ingredients. Is this the authentic YOU? What points of view have you accepted that don't sit well with you? What questions are in your mind that you have not even scratched the **surface** to **deeply** examine to get the answers to? What do you want? What is for you and awaiting your arrival? Are you willing to resist the opposition? Certainly, in life, there are many opposing forces. Some of these forces cause you to be stationary and not move forward; you're stuck. Some opposing forces give us the trajectory of moving at a constant speed, and depending on which is the driving force can cause us to constantly move forward or backward. In which direction are you moving? Also, there are opposing forces that become unbalanced because of friction which will cause you to be derailed.

I would like to propose to you that you allow the gift, the calling, the ember or the fire within you, the dream, the idea, the will to win, the determination, the courage, or the tenacity, to be the engine, the force that catapults you into attaining your success and authentically ***be***ing the new you, the better you, the refined you, the unapologetic you who said it can be done.

Defiance against a rule, an expectation, a belief, or any limitation is not always a bad thing. It's ***the power of You***. With grit, Determination and courage, tap into the power of *you* and ignite the flame that sets you apart from the rest. Defy Limits.

Trouble the waters, change the tide, shift the atmosphere, speak to the wind and fight against the pull of opposing forces. ***Be an opposing force to the opposing forces.***

DEFY LIMITS & ROCK YOUR MOXIE!

Birthings of Thought

Season 4

Up out of the Ashes
Resurrection

Another emergence. Another victory. Newness of life is your portion. You have risen from the stench of dead and dark matter. You have yet another chance to show up in this world and be the authentic You, intentionally and on purpose.

This is the season of breakthrough, to break forth, to rise above, to take flight and soar in your life. You've soldiered on and you're still here. You may have been bruised, cut, torn and your bones may have been broken, but the scars from your wounds and your limp will only serve as a reminder of your darkest and fiery experiences in life. Initially, in this season, the stench of the fire is on you, or you've broken through the shell of what was your prison and safe place and your wings are still wet and too heavy to fly. Understand that you've been through a lot and you're not done yet.

This is a season of maturity that brings clarity, understanding, wisdom, the ability to shift your perspective to what is true, honest, lovely, of a good report and virtuous—bringing honor to your legacy and a compass for the people who are reading *your* book, whether your book is forming in real time or already written.

Throughout our lives, we experience many ups and downs. We have a tendency to remember the bad, unfortunate, negative and hurting moments of our lives more than the good. We allow the negative things to form our way of thinking and also allow those unfortunate things to shape us, many times unaware that we don't allow them to work out for our good as they are intended to do. We often notice and focus on the opposing forces and accept them as limitations rather than allowing ourselves to be stretched by resisting them. We often become bitter, unforgiving, untrusting, skeptical and negative; thus, stunting our growth and allowing ourselves to live the balance of our lives in a rut and not living a meaningful life.

Case in Point 1: A lady can be in a relationship with someone who demeans her, beats her, leaves her with physical, emotional and mental scars which can make her believe she is worthless and that her life is pointless. Instead of removing herself from this toxicity, even though she has had the revelations and epiphanies that she is worth so much more and has so much more to offer, she remains and continues to be stripped, which will eventually affect her spiritually because God has given her a precious and purposeful gift that is her responsibility.

We can go to therapy, hire a coach, listen to podcasts, read blogs, watch ministries and motivational speakers on YouTube, plead the blood of Jesus, quote scriptures, fast and pray. But staying in a toxic environment becomes a contagion to us if we don't detox. It's like knowing there's a radiation leak, yet you stay in the environment knowing that exposure to deadly elements will lead to imminent death, assuming that God is not going to allow any deadly thing to harm you and ignoring the way of escape offered to you. This is a case of being home, a place of toxic normalcy, a place of familiarity, a place of average and mediocrity, a place where you crash, burn and are consumed.

The Question Is…

My pastor, Bishop Ronald Stephens, is a great leader who asks great questions. When he talks to me, I know he will reveal his query. I always brace myself with anticipation because I know he will require me to investigate myself and stretch me after our encounter. I first met and spoke with him on the Sunday he was consecrated and installed as pastor of Temple Church of Christ. I approached him and offered congratulations and he warmly obliged. At that moment, I realized he knew who I was. Now, I was surprised he knew and had an impression and perception of who I was. After he greeted me and said thank you, he immediately gave me accolades (which completely humbled me) and then asked, "Lady E, how do you know when you've arrived… How does it feel to have arrived?" The question baffled me. He continued with the exploits of my ministry of song, my voice, the projects I had released that were being played on all of the local Gospel radio stations and my reputation. I collected myself and answered, "Pastor Stephens, I don't know how it feels or what it's like to arrive. I don't believe anyone has arrived. I believe when we arrive, our work here on Earth is done, because as long as we are living, there is opportunity for growth and lessons to learn. He seemed impressed, and, honestly, I was impressed because I was still getting to know the organic me.

Bishop Stephens became my pastor after my husband and I got married. As a pastor who cares about those who are under his tutelage, the pastor and I have had many conversations that left me thinking and searching beyond the surface. Here's one conversation we had several years ago that afforded me the opportunity to have a total recall of my life within seconds when he asked me this question that was daunting and somewhat exhilarating at the same time. He passively forced me to answer this question. While responding, I not only heard but also listened to my response. At that moment, my perception and perspective of everything I believed and the person I had become was called into self-review.

The Question Was…

Q: On a scale of 1 to 10, overall, 1 being the lowest and 10 being your apex, where are you in life?

As I pondered and searched deeply, strangely, this question felt invasive, yet, intuitively, I knew I was being summoned to have an unintentional IMAGERY moment. I was apprehended because, at that moment, I was reluctant to dig ***deep*** because *my truth* was about to become *my power,* and not only did I *not* want to go ***deep,*** I was also apprehensive of the answer because I didn't want to expose my *weakness* to him or reinforce it to myself. It was necessary for me to take a very *pregnant* pause to think before answering. I intuitively knew this was not just a conversational, run-of-the-mill, surface inquiry. I would have to go ***deep*** to answer truthfully. Finally, I broke the silence with my truth which left me with mixed emotions.

A: "A six and a half (6.5) or seven (7)."

Why did a 6.5 – 7.0 make me feel good? Because 20 years before this encounter ensued, I would have rated myself a zero (0) or one (1). Ten years before, it probably would have been a three (3), and five (5) years ago, it would have definitely been a strong solid five (5). The pregnant pause caused me to take a look in the rearview mirror to review my past, my mindset, the process, my journey and the race I was running. As I answered, there was a sense that I'd fallen short and was not good enough, yet there was a greater sense of accomplishment. I recognized change, growth and metamorphosis. I realized that, even though I wanted to say a higher number, the 6.5-7 was a movement forward and in the right direction.

Why did 6.5 – 7.0 make me *not* feel good enough? Because I couldn't honestly say ten (10). Because I knew I had dropped the ball on myself and had setbacks and paralyzing limiting beliefs (in myself), and multiple times I had quit, dared not dream or was derailed because I was cowardly and fearful of failing along this journey and in most cases didn't know my worth or believe I was capable of accomplishing anything. I would rather do nothing than settle for mediocrity. I am not wired to do less than or just enough to get by or to be average. I am wired to go all in or nothing at all.

Why am I sharing this with you? Because, though you're in this season of Resurrection and rising from the flames out of the ashes, you too may be able to identify with my angst to identify where you are on a scale of 1-10.

Looking in the rearview mirror is not turning back to face your past; it's continuing in forward motion and seeing how far you've come as you're moving forward.

The challenge in the question is to look back in retrospect, not getting caught up in the emotional attachment of your past while utilizing a rearview mirror introspection. Looking in the rearview mirror is not turning back to face your past; it's continuing in forward motion and seeing how far you've come as you're moving forward. Any progress made, large or miniscule is still progress unless you've applied the brakes and stopped. In this season of resurrection, where are you in every area of your life, on a scale of 1-10?

You have lived, learned, developed, grown, been imprisoned, crashed, burned and risen from the ashes. This is the season of absolution, breathing again and starting over with a fresh perspective for your remaining days on this Earth. *You* know that it's ok to dream, execute and accomplish. The vision *you* saw in your mind that has synced with your heart that you don't yet see is manifesting and coming to fruition. What you once said was a lost cause, *you* now know is not only a possibility, but it is absolute. *You* now revel in the thrill of victory, understanding there are impending struggles, but you know that *you* have in you everything you need. *You* now know how to discern, pivot, shift and make sweet out of sour. With anticipation, *you* even look forward to some of the challenges in life just to prove to the opposing forces that you can still rise to the challenge and have the thrill of victory.

Even though physically, gravity is taking place, it is to be appreciated because you're still standing upright. This is the season for adding value to others with the wisdom that has been cultivated to bring forth the organic and authentic you. Looking out for those who played an integral part in every stage you've been through and understanding the stages they were going through when they didn't serve you well, thus being astute in recognizing the grade of their organic soil.

This is the final call. Giving up after all you've been through is not an option. There are bucket lists to check off, visions to cast, dreams to realize, ideas to pitch and people to pour into. Watch your mindset. Opposing voices will speak to you subconsciously. Remember, what happened before your resurrection really did happen and left imprints (tattoos). It is too easy to go back to the familiar.

Stay Aware

The World is still ***Your*** oyster. The grit and irritations of this world are unrelenting, and until *you* are complete, made perfect and entire. Remain steadfast, unmovable and abound, ***Be***ing *You*. Display the pearl you have ***Be***come.

You've done this before and if you choose to remember this you will master every season to come. Congratulate yourself on your ability to remain viable and on your graduation from then to now. What's next?

Birthings of Thought, Ahas, and Revelations

Conclusion

You... Are A Purposeful Gift

You are clothed in skin, flesh, muscle, fat, sinew and bone. All of that will eventually decay. However, inside of it all lies a treasure in an earthen vessel.

Question: What keeps you from unwrapping or unveiling this gift? The gift is not useful to anyone if you don't unwrap it. More importantly, it is not useful to you if you are not willing to open it up and release it. Suppressed promise and potential is useful to no one. If it is housed in a decaying wrapping, it's not being released to whomever needs to receive it and it will not survive your decay. There's no legacy when you're gone, no keepsake, no significant remembrance.

First things first, ***YOU*** must see beyond the ***surface*** or veil of your flesh or skin (your superficial self or how you are perceived by others), your limiting beliefs (beliefs that keep you from living out loud) and lies you've been told and believe: perception, perspective, point of view.

If what you see (your perception) is an optical illusion, your gift will never be useful to you or anyone else and you will have influenced those who are attached to you to keep their gift under wraps.

What hinders you?

Momma said–Daddy said–sibling said–husband said–teacher said–friends said–boss said

I was taught–I experienced–I saw–I have never–I can't because–I don't know

If your gift is God's purpose for your life, who's the liar? Them or God?

Are you taking dictation from a lie and writing it in your heart?

There's a fire in your belly!

How do you know that what's in your belly is Purposeful?

If you have had this dream, desire or idea for years and it burns as much now as it did 10 years ago. It needs to be explored and pursued.

If you started and circumstances and distractions got in the way, and it's been partially unwrapped and you gave up or lost your momentum, look back in retrospect and don't think you were a failure because you weren't successful. Don't blame it on the distractions in life, but ***Still Dream*** of a more favorable outcome. You can still see it and the fire still burns.

Go to your quiet place, look in the mirror, start talking yourself into unwrapping the present, the gift of ***You***!

Epilogue

It is true that we become comfortable with discomfort. For Christians, living in the will of God is not a death sentence. Non-believers see life's drama as being unlucky, karma, or a reason to say there is no God.

Below are excerpts from the Holy Bible, a book that is a compilation of books that hundreds of millions of people have in their homes and contents hidden in their hearts. It is the #1 Bestselling book of all time. There has to be something to it as it is not categorized as fictional. Rather it is spiritual, history, poetry, biographical, bibliographical, instructional, inspirational, self-help and nonfiction; it is translated in 704 languages with many versions. Here are just a few verses of scripture for reference of what the irrefutable ink of God says about you as well as instructions and promises in His book.

Psalms 139:13,14 (NKJV)
For You formed my inward parts;
You covered me in my mother's womb.
I will praise You, for **I am fearfully *and* wonderfully made**;

Marvelous are Your works,
And *that* my soul knows very well.

John 10:10 (NKJV)
The thief does not come except to steal, and to kill, and to destroy.
I have come that they may have life, and that they may have *it* more abundantly.

Proverbs 10:22 (NKJV)
The blessing of the Lord makes *one* rich,
And He adds no sorrow with it.

Ephesians 3:20 (AMP)
Now to Him who is able to [carry out His purpose and] do superabundantly more than all that we dare ask or think [infinitely beyond our greatest prayers, hopes, or dreams], according to His power that is at work within us

1 Corinthians 2:9 (MSG)
We, of course, have plenty of wisdom to pass on to you once you get your feet on firm spiritual ground, but it's not popular wisdom, the fashionable wisdom of high-priced experts that will be out-of-date in a year or so. God's wisdom is something mysterious that goes deep into the interior of his purposes. You don't find it lying around on the surface. It's not the latest message, but more like the oldest—what God determined as the way to bring out his

best in us, long before we ever arrived on the scene. The experts of our day haven't a clue about what this eternal plan is. If they had, they wouldn't have killed the Master of the God-designed life on a cross. That's why we have this Scripture text: No one's ever seen or heard anything like this, Never so much as imagined anything quite like it— What God has arranged for those who love him. But *you've* seen and heard it because God by his Spirit has brought it all out into the open before you. The Spirit, not content to flit around on the surface, dives into the depths of God, and brings out what God planned all along. Who ever knows what you're thinking and planning except yourself? The same with God—except that he not only knows what he's thinking, but he lets *us* in on it. God offers a full report on the gifts of life and salvation that he is giving us. We don't have to rely on the world's guesses and opinions. We didn't learn this by reading books or going to school; we learned it from God, who taught us person-to-person through Jesus, and we're passing it on to you in the same firsthand, personal way.

Psalms 23 (KJV)

The Lord is my shepherd; I shall not want.

He maketh me to lie down in green pastures: he leadeth me beside the still waters.

He restoreth my soul: he leadeth me in the paths of righteousness for his name's sake.

Yea, though I walk through the valley of the shadow of death, I will fear no evil: for thou art with me; thy rod and thy staff they comfort me.
Thou preparest a table before me in the presence of mine enemies: thou anointest my head with oil; my cup runneth over.
Surely goodness and mercy shall follow me all the days of my life: and I will dwell in the house of the Lord forever.

Phillipians 4:7 (KJV)
And the peace of God, which passeth all understanding, shall keep your hearts and minds through Christ Jesus.

Isaiah 26:3 (AMP)
"You will keep in perfect *and* constant peace *the one* whose mind is steadfast [that is, committed and focused on You—in both inclination and character], Because he trusts *and* takes refuge in You [with hope and confident expectation].

Phillipians 4:13 (AMP)
I can do all things [which He has called me to do] through Him who strengthens *and* empowers me [to fulfill His purpose—I am self-sufficient in Christ's sufficiency; I am ready for anything and equal to anything through Him who infuses me with inner strength and confident peace.]

Hebrews 10:35 (AMP)

Do not, therefore, fling away your [fearless] confidence, for it has a glorious *and* great reward.

Author Bio

Eneazer Layne is the founder of IMAGERY International Movement, the "I AM" Movement, a not-for-profit Women's Empowerment Organization, launched with the purpose to pour, encourage and empower girls and women of all ages.

For over 40 years, Lady E has found joy in being a source of transformative inspiration to countless young ladies coming into womanhood, as well as women of all ages. Layne operates Awakened Consciousness Coaching, Empowerment & Speaking Services (ACCESS) and Defy Limits, adding value by challenging mindsets, expanding beliefs and uplifting and encouraging women to Rock Their Moxie! Layne is also a proud member of The John Maxwell Team, offering masterclasses, and coaching for individuals and organizations in growth, leadership and life.

Book Summary

Surface Deep...The Evolution of You is an unfiltered and enlightened guide to digging deeper to bring forth the best you possible. Rooted in faith and personal stories of triumphs and overcoming tribulations, the book was written from an anatomical and physiological perspective to activate you to live everything between your birth and death with purpose, determination and without limits.

Surface Deep is an excellent tool for women's groups, ministries and book clubs. Inquire at www.surfacedeepbook.com to receive information on when and how to get the *Surface Deep* workbook to expand your perspective and reach breakthroughs to become the best version of yourself.

Surface Deep is book one of volumes to come.

CPSIA information can be obtained
at www.ICGtesting.com
Printed in the USA
BVHW021814020922
646141BV00020B/962